MW00668586

Getting in Shape

for Violin

by Cassia Harvey

edited by Judith Harvey

CHP123
ISBN **978-1-932823-22-6**

6403 N. 6th Street
Philadelphia, PA 19126
www.charveypublications.com

Less-advanced (A) pages are structured so that they can be played together with more-advanced (B) pages.

Contents

Getting in Shape

Finger Trainer (A)

Cassia Harvey

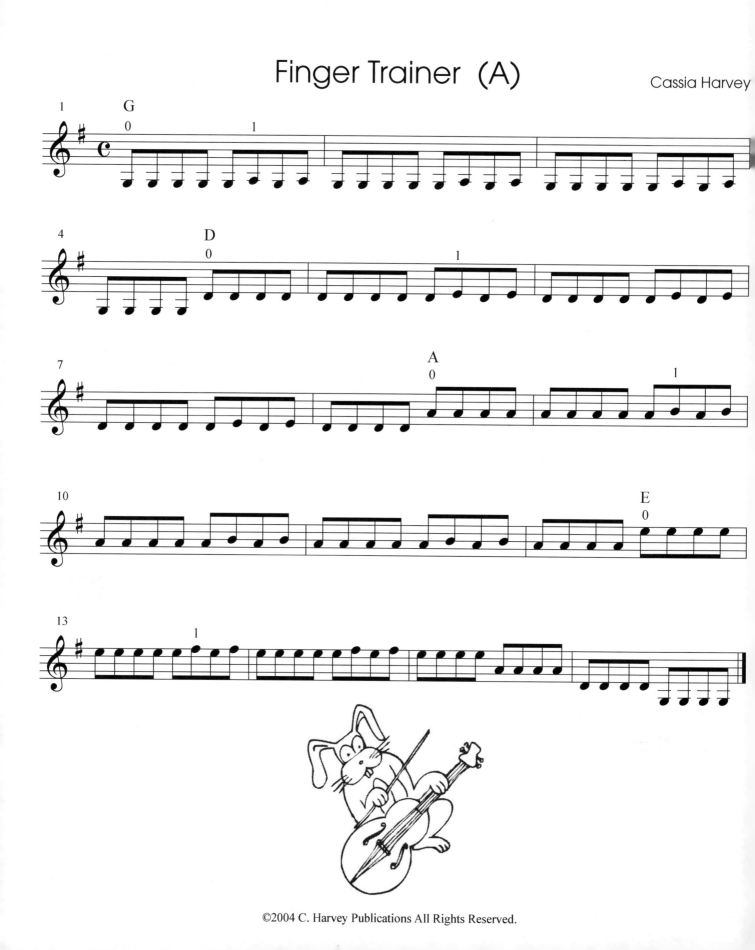

Little Brown Jug (A)

Trad./arr. C. Harvey

Test w/ Open strings often

Slow!

Finger Trainer (B)

Cassia Harvey

Use Elbow!

Little Brown Jug (B)

Trad./arr. C. Harvey

6

Finger Workout (A)

Cassia Harvey

Soldier's Chorus (A)

Bizet/arr. C. Harvey

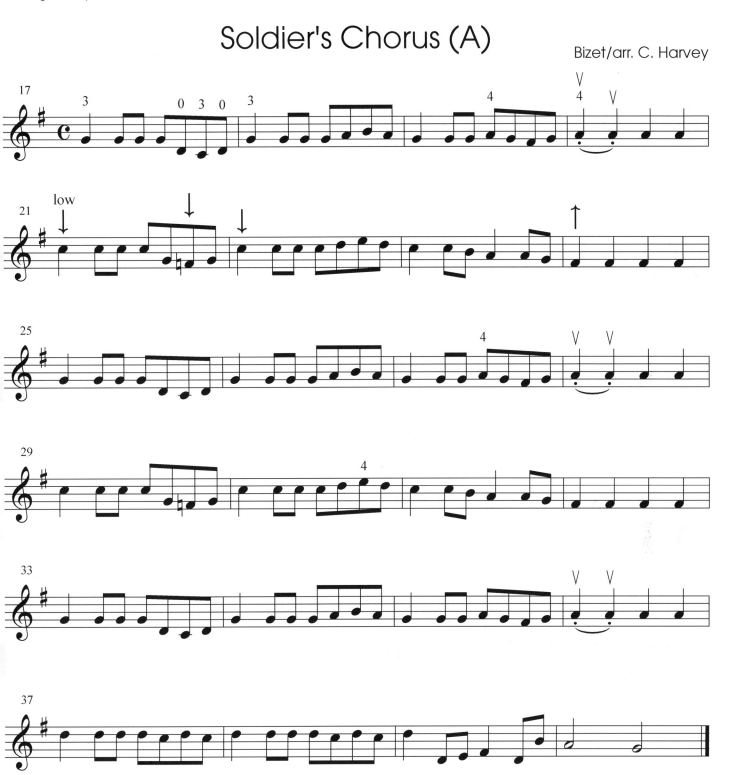

8

Finger Workout (B)

Cassia Harvey

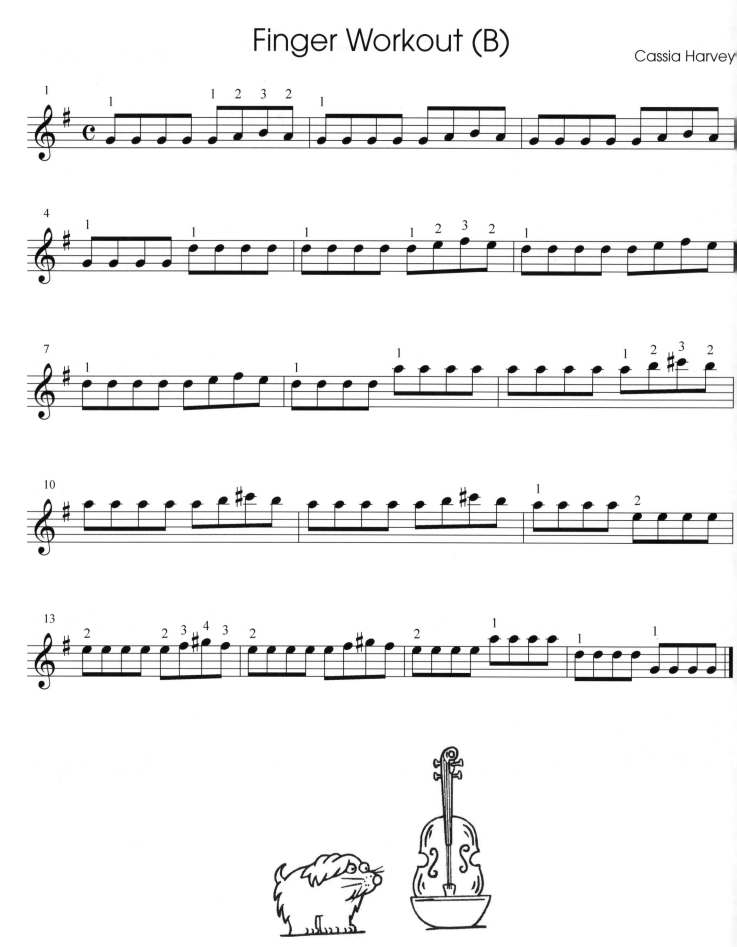

Soldier's Chorus (B)

Bizet/arr. C. Harvey

Daily Exercise (A)

Cassia Harvey

The Frog Went A-Courting (A)

Trad./arr. C. Harvey

Daily Exercise (B)

Cassia Harvey

The Frog Went A-Courting (B)

Trad./arr. C. Harvey

Finger and Bow Workout (A)

Cassia Harvey

Turkish Dance (A)

Kruckow/arr. C. Harvey

Finger and Bow Workout (B)

Cassia Harvey

Turkish Dance (B)

Kruckow/arr. C. Harvey

18

Pre-Skipping (A)

Cassia Harvey

Hopak (A)

Mussorgsky/arr. C. Harvey

feels slow

Pre-Skipping (B)

Cassia Harvey

Hopak (B)

Mussorgsky/arr. C. Harvey

Skipping (A)

Cassia Harvey

Brandenburg 5 (A)

Bach/arr. C. Harvey

24

Skipping (B)

Cassia Harvey

Brandenburg 5 (B)

Bach/arr. C. Harvey

26

Strength Exercise (A)

Cassia Harvey

Mairi's Wedding (A)

Trad./arr. C. Harvey

Strength Exercise (B)

Cassia Harvey

Mairi's Wedding (B)

Trad./arr. C. Harvey

Exercise for Both Hands (A/B)

Cassia Harvey

Karobushka (A/B)

Trad./arr. C. Harvey

Pre-Skipping (A)

Cassia Harvey

Fireworks Music (A)

Handel/arr. C. Harvey

Pre-Skipping (B)

Cassia Harvey

Fireworks Music (B)

Handel/arr. C. Harvey

Skipping (A)

Cassia Harvey

Arkansas Traveler (A)

Trad./arr. C. Harvey

38

Skipping (B)

Cassia Harvey

1

2

Arkansas Traveler (B)

Trad./arr. C. Harvey

First Position Workout (A)

Cassia Harvey

High Cap (A)

Trad./arr. C. Harvey

First Position Workout (B)

Cassia Harvey

High Cap (B)

Trad./arr. C. Harvey

Pre-Skipping (A)

Cassia Harvey

Pickles for Breakfast (A)

Trad./arr. C. Harvey

Pre-Skipping (B)

Cassia Harvey

Pickles for Breakfast (B)

Trad./arr. C. Harvey

48

Skipping (A)

Cassia Harvey

Chicken on the Fence Post (A)

Trad./arr. C. Harvey

Skipping (B)

Cassia Harvey

Chicken on the Fence Post (B)

Trad./arr. C. Harvey

First Position Workout (A)

Cassia Harvey

Flower Song (A)

Trad./arr. C. Harvey

First Position Workout (B)

Cassia Harvey

Flower Song (B)

Trad./arr. C. Harvey

Skipping (A)

Cassia Harvey

The British Grenadiers (A)

Trad./arr. C. Harvey

58

Skipping (B)

Cassia Harvey

The British Grenadiers (B)

Trad. /arr. C. Harvey

Third Position for the Violin, Book One

Cassia Harvey

First Shifting on the A string

First Shifting on the E string

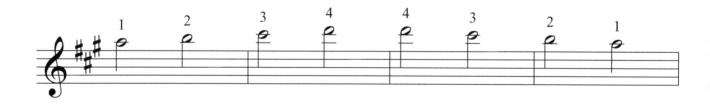

60307086R00035

Made in the USA
Columbia, SC
13 June 2019